EVOLUTION

THE LAST DAYS OF THE DINOSAURS

The incredible
story of
life on Earth

145 to 66 million years ago

Thanks to the creative team:

Senior Editor: Alice Peebles

Designer: Lauren Woods and
collaborate agency

Consultant: Paolo Viscardi

First published in Great Britain in 2015
by Hungry Tomato Ltd

PO Box 181

Edenbridge

Kent, TN8 9DP

A CIP catalogue record for this book is available
from the British Library.

ISBN 978-1-910684-02-3

Printed and bound in China

Discover more at
www.hungrytomato.com

THE LAST DAYS OF THE DINOSAURS

By Matthew Rake

Illustrated by Pete Minister

HUNGRY TOMATO™

Everything alive
today is related to
life from the past.

CONTENTS

mya means 'million years ago'

THE LAST DAYS OF
THE DINOSAURS

THE LAST DAYS OF THE DINOSAURS

Hi, My name is Ackerley and I'm an acanthostega.

I'm your guide in this book and I have got the world's greatest story to tell you – how life evolved on Earth. Or to put it another way...

...how we all got here.

This is the third book in the series. In the first two, The Dawn of Planet Earth and Dinosaurs Rule, we found out how tiny organisms - so small you need a microscope to see them - evolved into huge dinosaurs.

But in this book, things really get scary. It covers the Cretaceous period, when dinosaurs as big as tanks and flying reptiles as big as fighter jets dominated the world. We'll find out, for example, how tyrannosaurus rex had teeth bigger than bananas and used them to bite with a force like no other land animal.

Mind you, T. rex wasn't the biggest meat-eating dinosaur. That title goes to spinosaurus, a dinosaur with a head like a crocodile's and a sail on its back! It may have weighed an astonishing 21,000kg - that's the same as 30 Formula 1 cars, plus all their drivers.

How do we know this stuff?

Scientists who study the history of living things are known as palaeontologists. To learn about life in the past, they find and study fossils. Fossils are simply the remains of animals and plants that have been preserved in rocks.

There are two types of fossil: body fossils and trace fossils. A body fossil preserves the actual parts of an animal or plant. A trace fossil preserves the marks that organisms have made. For example, an animal may have made a burrow or footprints, or a plant may have left holes where its roots once were.

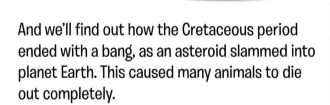

I'll also tell you about some of the more gentle Cretaceous creatures: how centrosaurs travelled in huge herds of 1,000 or more across North America, and how maiasura fed and took care of their young.

And we'll find out how the Cretaceous period ended with a bang, as an asteroid slammed into planet Earth. This caused many animals to die out completely.

In the fourth book of the series, The Rise of the Mammals, we'll look at how this set of animals evolved to dominate the planet, including some that were every bit as scary as the dinosaurs.

Changing Shape of the Planet

You may think the map of the world has always looked the same. But the continents have changed dramatically throughout the history of Earth, just as animals and plants have. About 225 million years ago, the whole world was one big supercontinent called Pangaea.

About 225 million years ago

About 200 million years ago, the continent of Pangaea was dividing into Laurasia in the north and Gondwanaland in the south.

About 200 million years ago

By 65 million years ago, when the dinosaurs were wiped out, the world was looking much more like it does today. Laurasia was splitting up into North America in the west and Europe and Asia in the east. Gondwanaland had split into South America, Africa, India and Antarctica/Australia.

About 65 million years ago

In the last 65 million years, North and South America have joined up, Antarctica and Australia separated, and India merged with the continent of Asia.

EVOLUTION TIMELINE

The story begins with the Big Bang 15,000 million years ago (mya). Life on Earth starts around 3,800 mya. Oxygen forms in the atmosphere about 2,300 mya as a waste product of photosynthesizing bacteria, in what scientists call the Great Oxygenation Event. The ozone layer begins forming above the Earth 600 mya - this will eventually protect the Earth from the harmful rays of the sun. These events mean that animals will ultimately be able to live on land.

The first reptiles evolve from one branch of amphibians. Reptiles are the first animals with backbones to live permanently on land. Vast forests cover the land, and these will eventually fossilize and become coal.

Sea animals start appearing in the 'Cambrian explosion of life' 540-520 mya. They swim, crawl, burrow, hunt, defend themselves and hide away. Some creatures evolve hard parts such as shells.

Life begins on land, as plants grow by lakes, streams and coasts, and arthropods (animals with segmented bodies like millipedes) venture onto land. The first jawed fish appear.

Precambrian

Cambrian

Devonian

Carboniferous

Precambrian 4,540-541 mya	Cambrian 541-485 mya	Ordovician 485-443 mya	Silurian 443-419 mya	Devonian 419-359 mya	Carboniferous 359-299 mya

The 'golden age of the dinosaurs'

witnesses huge herbivore dinosaurs feeding on lush ferns and palm-like cycads. Smaller but vicious meat-eating dinosaurs hunt the great herbivores.

Homo sapiens appear

in Africa around 200,000 years ago. By 40,000 years ago, they also live in Europe, southern Asia and Australia. Around 16,000 years ago, they move into North America.

Dinosaurs appear,

as do the first mammals and the first flying animals with backbones, the pterosaurs.

Many different mammals evolve –

some stay on land; some, like whales, go back into the water; some, like monkeys, take to the trees.

Triassic

Jurassic

Cretaceous

Paleogene

Neogene

Quaternary

Permian 299-252 mya	Triassic 252-201 mya	Jurassic 201-145 mya	Cretaceous 145-66 mya	Paleogene 66-23 mya	Neogene 23-2.6 mya	Quaternary 2.6 mya - now

BATTLE ON THE BANK

Why did **spinosaurus** have a sail on its back? Like the peacock's tail, it might have helped to attract mates. Or like an elephant's ears, it might have been used to control its body temperature. It is unlikely that the sail was needed for deterring enemies because, at around 15 metres (49ft) long, spinosaurus wouldn't have had many.

Spinosaurus

Spinosaurus is probably the largest of all known carnivorous dinosaurs, even larger than tyrannosaurus rex and giganotosaurus. The problem is, no complete spinosaurus skeleton has been found, so scientists can't be absolutely sure!

Sarcosuchus

This **spinosaurus** likes to go down to the river for a drink and a bite to eat, and they may have been semiaquatic. It could easily pick fish out with its long, thin snout. Well, today it has picked out a bit more than he bargained for. Half-submerged among the reeds is **sarcosuchus**, the biggest crocodile ever known. They may have had the biggest fight in the history of the planet.

So who will win this epic battle? If sarcosuchus can gets its massive jaws into the neck of spinosaurus, it can use its low centre of gravity to bring down spinosaurus and drown it underwater. It's a move that today's crocs use. It is a big "if" though! Spinosaurus towers over sarcosuchus and could do some damage to the supercroc's neck first.

SARCOSUCHUS
Location: Rivers of Africa
Length: 12 metres (39ft 5in)

Precambrian 4,540-541mya	
Cambrian 541-485mya	
Ordovician 485-443 mya	
Silurian 443-419 mya	
Devonian 419-359 mya	
Carboniferous 359-299mya	
Permian 299-252mya	
Triassic 252-201mya	
Jurassic 201-145mya	

Cretaceous 145-66mya

Paleogene 66-23mya	
Neogene 23-2.6mya	
Quaternary 2.6mya - present	

I'm staying well out the way of this one. About 110 million years ago, North Africa was home to some of the biggest carnivores ever – and the two most dangerous were spinosaurus and the supercroc, sarcosuchus. Basically, they are both the size of very big buses.

If there were boxing promoters in those days, they'd be calling this the "Thriller in the River", "War in the Water"- or - perhaps the "Battle on the Bank".

Did You Know?
The biggest modern croc ever measured was Lolong, a saltwater crocodile living in captivity in the Philippines until he died in 2013. He was 6.17 metres (20ft 3in) long and weighed 1,075kg (2,370lb). Sarcosuchus was about eight times heavier and twice the length of Lolong.

HUNTING IN PACKS

You'd think **tenontosaurus** would have been able to look after itself, wouldn't you? It was a peace-loving vegetarian, but it measured 8 metres (26ft) long and 3 metres (10ft) high. And it weighed in at about 2 tonnes – that's about

25 times heavier than deinonychus.

However, for a pack of deinonychus, tenontosaurus's massive size meant it was just a nice, juicy main course.

Deinonychus was a swift, agile meat-eating dinosaur. Scientists believe its favourite meal was **tenontosaurus** because its teeth and skeletons have often been discovered next to tenontosaurus remains.

Tenontosaurus

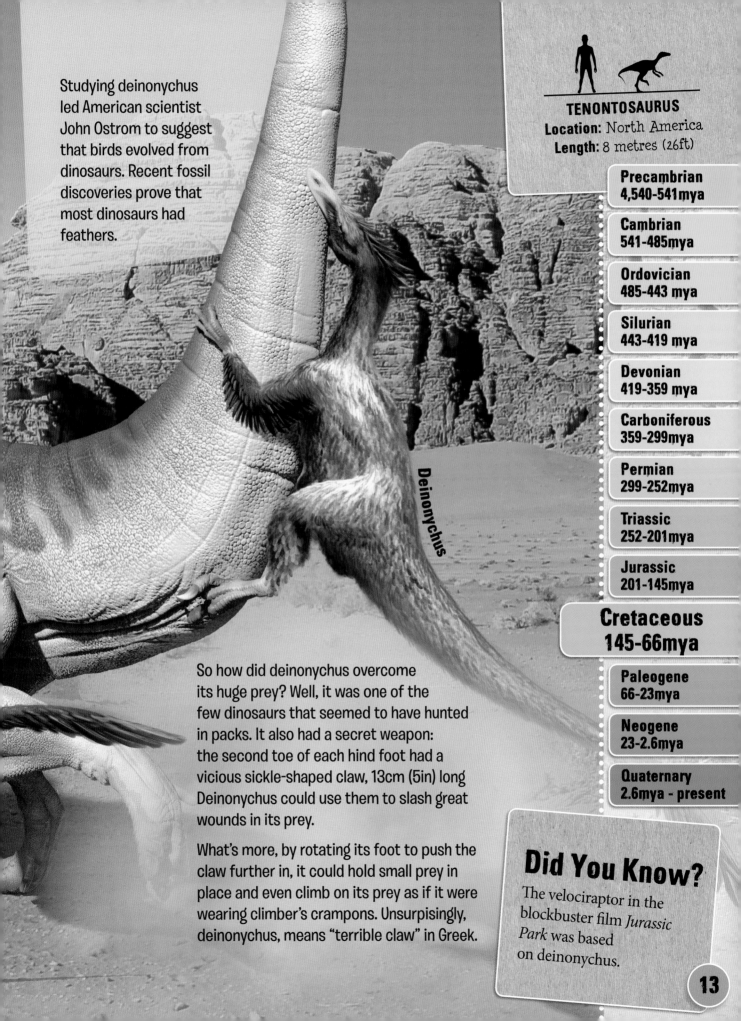

Studying deinonychus led American scientist John Ostrom to suggest that birds evolved from dinosaurs. Recent fossil discoveries prove that most dinosaurs had feathers.

Deinonychus

So how did deinonychus overcome its huge prey? Well, it was one of the few dinosaurs that seemed to have hunted in packs. It also had a secret weapon: the second toe of each hind foot had a vicious sickle-shaped claw, 13cm (5in) long Deinonychus could use them to slash great wounds in its prey.

What's more, by rotating its foot to push the claw further in, it could hold small prey in place and even climb on its prey as if it were wearing climber's crampons. Unsurprisingly, deinonychus, means "terrible claw" in Greek.

TENONTOSAURUS
Location: North America
Length: 8 metres (26ft)

| Precambrian 4,540-541mya |
| Cambrian 541-485mya |
| Ordovician 485-443 mya |
| Silurian 443-419 mya |
| Devonian 419-359 mya |
| Carboniferous 359-299mya |
| Permian 299-252mya |
| Triassic 252-201mya |
| Jurassic 201-145mya |

Cretaceous 145-66mya

| Paleogene 66-23mya |
| Neogene 23-2.6mya |
| Quaternary 2.6mya - present |

Did You Know?

The velociraptor in the blockbuster film *Jurassic Park* was based on deinonychus.

BIG BEASTS

Diplodocus, at 30 metres (43ft), was the longest dinosaur but it looked like a lightweight next to dreadnoughtus.

In 2014, scientists announced the discovery of the biggest dinosaur ever to have roamed the Earth. They called it dreadnoughtus, after a fearsome World War I battleship. Dreadnought is from early English and means "fear nothing".

The specimen was found in 2005 in Patagonia, Argentina. As the find was in a remote region and the bones were so big, it took four years to excavate the remains.

Then it took palaeontologists five years to study the bones, reconstruct them into one skeleton and publish the results of their findings.

The specimen was 26 metres (85ft) lon,g with an 11-metre (37ft) neck and 9-metre (30ft) tail. And get this, it wasn't even a fully grown adult. Scientists knew this because its shoulder bones had not yet fused together, which would have happened in an adult of its type.

Check out this monster. It's the sauropod dinosaur dreadnoughtus and it weighed 60,000kg (65 tons) – or to put it another way, the equivalent of twelve African elephants, seven T. rexes, two and a half diplodocuses or one Boeing 737 (with passengers and baggage on board!)

Here you can see how it shapes up against giganotosaurus and another sauropod, diplodocus. Scientists think giganotosaurus, which also lived in Argentina, was the second biggest meat-eating dinosaur ever. The biggest meat-eater? See pages 10-11 to find this out.

And no, it's not T. rex.

Diplodocus

26m
22m
20m
18m
16m
14m
12m
8m
6m
4m
2m

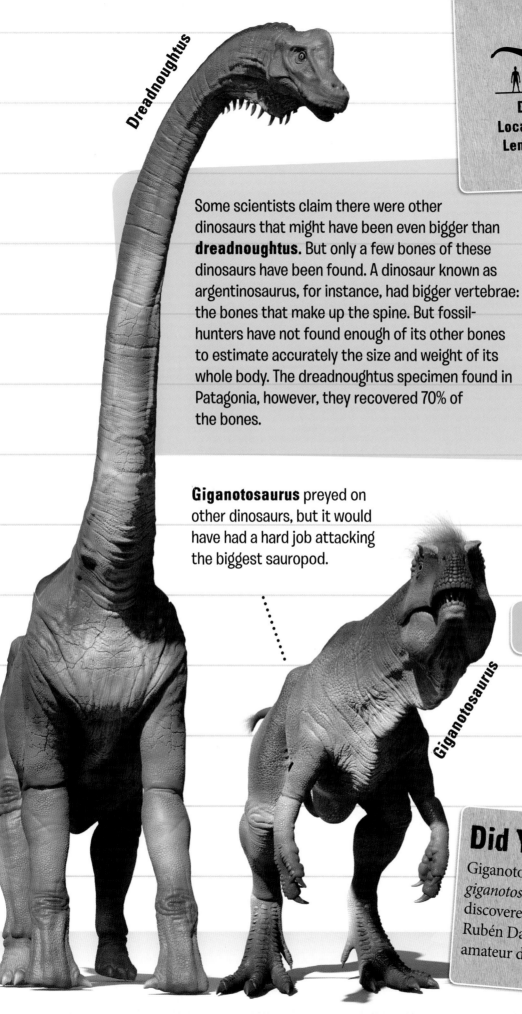

Dreadnoughtus

Some scientists claim there were other dinosaurs that might have been even bigger than **dreadnoughtus.** But only a few bones of these dinosaurs have been found. A dinosaur known as argentinosaurus, for instance, had bigger vertebrae: the bones that make up the spine. But fossil-hunters have not found enough of its other bones to estimate accurately the size and weight of its whole body. The dreadnoughtus specimen found in Patagonia, however, they recovered 70% of the bones.

Giganotosaurus preyed on other dinosaurs, but it would have had a hard job attacking the biggest sauropod.

Giganotosaurus

Precambrian
4,540-541mya

Cambrian
541-485mya

Ordovician
485-443 mya

Silurian
443-419 mya

Devonian
419-359 mya

Carboniferous
359-299mya

Permian
299-252mya

Triassic
252-201mya

Jurassic
201-145mya

Cretaceous
145-66mya

Paleogene
66-23mya

Neogene
23-2.6mya

Quaternary
2.6mya - present

Did You Know?

Giganotosaurus - full name *giganotosaurus carolini* - was discovered and named after Rubén Dario Carolini, an amateur dinosaur hunter.

PREHISTORIC HANG-GLIDERS

Imagine a creature as tall as a giraffe when on the ground, and with the wingspan of a fighter jet when in the air. Meet quetzalcoatlus, the largest flying creature that ever existed.

Quetzalcoatlus was a type of flying reptile known as a pterosaur. Pterosaurs emerged about 230 million years ago at the same time as the dinosaurs. And just like dinosaurs, as the pterosaurs evolved, they got bigger and bigger...

Quetzalcoatlus may have been lord of the skies 70 million years ago, but today nobody is quite sure how this enormous creature managed to get off the ground in the first place. Some scientists think it needed a cliff to jump off, or at least a downward slope to act as a runway. Others suggest it may have lost the ability to fly and adapted to living on land, like the modern ostrich.

What quetzalcoatlus ate is a mystery, too. Some believe it flew down to water and skimmed fish into its metre-long beak - yet it lived hundreds of kilometres from the seas. Others think its long, thin beak would have been perfect for poking deep inside carcasses - so maybe, like the vulture, it lived by scavenging. Or, perhaps like the modern storks it simply stalked small animals on land.

Like other pterosaurs, quetzalcoatlus walked on all fours on land, so would have been able to stalk its prey. And maybe those gigantic wings came in handy gathering up the prey. It might also have waded through shallow water, picking up fish, snails and shellfish in its giant beak. Although it did not have big feet, it may have had webbing between the toes to help spread its weight on sandy and muddy ground when walking.

QUETZALCOATLUS
Location: North America
Wingspan: 10-11 metres (33-36ft)

Precambrian	4,540-541mya
Cambrian	541-485mya
Ordovician	485-443 mya
Silurian	443-419 mya
Devonian	419-359 mya
Carboniferous	359-299mya
Permian	299-252mya
Triassic	252-201mya
Jurassic	201-145mya
Cretaceous	145-66mya
Paleogene	66-23mya
Neogene	23-2.6mya
Quaternary	2.6mya - present

Did You Know?
One study says this lord of the skies flew at speeds of up to 130 kph (80mph) for seven to 10 days non-stop, and at altitudes of 4,750 metres (15,000ft). Imagine that passing overhead!

17

CHILD'S PLAY

Unlike mammals, most reptiles wouldn't exactly win any Best Parenting Awards. They generally abandon their eggs after they have laid them. There are exceptions, of course. In your world, a few lizards and snakes guard their eggs: pythons incubate their eggs for a while, and crocodiles tend both the eggs and the hatchlings. But, check out the vegetarian maiasura –

they really did show the love.

In the 1970s, more than 200 specimens of **maiasaura** were found in what is now known as Egg Mountain formation, in western Montana, USA. The area was a nesting colony that these dinosaurs returned to year after year. They showed that maiasaura really cared for their kids.

At the colony, each mother would scrape out a nest in the ground and lay about 20 grapefruit-sized eggs. She didn't sit on the eggs to keep them warm, but brought rotting vegetation to cover them. As the nests were about 7 metres (23ft) apart, she could easily walk around without crushing the eggs.

The babies would be about 40cm (16in) when they hatched, and for the first months the mother would bring them plant shoots, leaves and berries to eat. A baby soon grew from the size of toaster to the size of tank.

Maiasaura babies

Maiasaura

MAIASAURA
Location: North America
Length: About 9 metres (30ft)

| Precambrian 4,540-541mya |
| Cambrian 541-485mya |
| Ordovician 485-443 mya |
| Silurian 443-419 mya |
| Devonian 419-359 mya |
| Carboniferous 359-299mya |
| Permian 299-252mya |
| Triassic 252-201mya |
| Jurassic 201-145mya |
| **Cretaceous 145-66mya** |
| Paleogene 66-23mya |
| Neogene 23-2.6mya |
| Quaternary 2.6mya - present |

Maiasura travelled in herds and scientists think they came back to the same safe place to nest every year. The nesting colony would have allowed them to protect their eggs and babies from predators, such as large lizards and meat-eating dinosaurs. And once they were big enough to leave the nest, the young would be protected as part of the herd.

IS IT A BIRD OR A DINOSAUR?

Protoceratops was quite vulnerable to predators. It had no armour and no horns, while the neck frill at the back of its skull was pretty frail. In fact, the frill was probably used to impress females rather than for protection. This makes some scientists think that protoceratops only dared come out at night. They point out that it had large eyes, which would have helped it to

see in the dark.

Other scientists believe it came out during the day, but only for short intervals.

Oviraptor

Oviraptor was a small bird-like dinosaur that lived in Asia about 80 million years ago. Like birds, it had a toothless beak and rigid ribcage, and was covered in feathers. No-one knows for sure what it lived on, but the shape of its beak suggests that it ate molluscs (for example, snails) and crustaceans (for example, crabs, lobsters and crayfish). Perhaps it also used its sharp beak to shred plants and break open fruit and nuts.

PROTOCERATOPS
Location: Asia
Length: 1.8 metres (6ft)

| Precambrian 4,540-541mya |
| Cambrian 541-485mya |
| Ordovician 485-443 mya |
| Silurian 443-419 mya |
| Devonian 419-359 mya |
| Carboniferous 359-299mya |
| Permian 299-252mya |
| Triassic 252-201mya |
| Jurassic 201-145mya |

Cretaceous 145-66mya

| Paleogene 66-23mya |
| Neogene 23-2.6mya |
| Quaternary 2.6mya - present |

Protoceratops

The name oviraptor is Latin for 'egg taker' or 'egg seizer'. It was given this name because the first oviraptor remains were found on top of a clutch of eggs that scientists thought belonged to protoceratops, a herbivorous dinosaur. The American scientist Henry Fairfield Osborn believed the oviraptor was trying to steal the eggs. In fact, scientists now think it was brooding a clutch of its own eggs in its nest. Instead of being an egg stealer, it was an egg protector!

Did You Know?

A protoceratops fossil being prepared for display in Poland in 2011 was found to have its footprint preserved in the rocks encasing the fossilized bones. Scientists think this is the only time one dinosaur's footprint and fossil have been found together.

MASS MOVEMENT

A few hundred years ago, bison used to migrate across North America in huge herds. But 75 million years before this, centrosaurs moved across the continent looking for the best plants to eat. Centrosaurs were bigger than bison and they travelled in herds of around 1,000 animals.

Just imagine it –

huge clouds of dust and the drumbeat of thousands and thousands of feet. It must have sounded like an earthquake and I reckon it would have frightened the fiercest meat-eating dinosaur.

Centrosaurus

In Alberta, Canada, entire **centrosaurus** herds, ranging from youngsters to old adults, have been found together in gigantic graves known as bone-beds. Scientists think many of these mass graves resulted from herds trying to cross flooded rivers. However, at one site, which contains no fewer than 14 mass graves, scientists think a huge hurricane must have blown in from the sea.

You can picture it: the skies darkening, the breeze picking up... and then suddenly, relentless rain, gale-force winds and seawater surging onto the land. As the waters rose, birds flew away, and small mammals and reptiles scurried up trees, and even took their chances at swimming. But the slow, dim-witted centrosaurs would have probably not noticed until it was too late. Anyway, where could they escape in the flat Canadian landscape?

CENTROSAURUS
Location: North America
Length: About 5 metres (20ft)

Precambrian 4,540-541mya
Cambrian 541-485mya
Ordovician 485-443 mya
Silurian 443-419 mya
Devonian 419-359 mya
Carboniferous 359-299mya
Permian 299-252mya
Triassic 252-201mya
Jurassic 201-145mya
Cretaceous 145-66mya
Paleogene 66-23mya
Neogene 23-2.6mya
Quaternary 2.6mya - present

Centrosaurus had many relatives in the centrosaurine family, all with different frills and horns on their skulls. Scientists think they all stayed with their own species, much like some of the different herds of grass-eaters on the African continent today. Impala, springbok and kudu, for example, all keep to their own species. By moving in herds, the animals can warn each other of danger and lessen their chances of being singled out by a predator.

Did You Know?
The name Centrosaurus means "pointed lizard" in Greek, and refers to the small horns on the edge of their frills, not to the front horn (which was unknown when the dinosaur was named).

ARMOURED DINOSAURS

There were many huge meat-eating dinosaurs in North America in the late Cretaceous period, including the king of dinosaurs, tyrannosaurus rex. But they needed to choose their prey carefully. Some of the plant-eating dinosaurs evolved defensive armour – and some, like ankylosaurus, could even fight back with a secret weapon.

Game on!

Ankylosaurus was essentially a prehistoric tank: 7 metres (23ft) long, heavily armoured and equipped with a lethal weapon. If a predator was not put off by those threatening spikes, it would soon wreck its teeth on the bite-proof bony plates that covered ankylosaurus's head, neck, back and tail.

Ankylosaurus

The only place to attack anklyosaurus was its soft underbelly. The trouble was, the creature weighed up to 7,000kg (7.7 tons) and was very low on the ground, so it would have been impossible to flip it over, even a T. rex couldn't have managed it. And any predator had better watch out, because ankylosaurus could swipe its tail viciously. This had a hard club at the end that was easily capable of breaking bones.

Styracosaurus (in the background here) was just as scary. It had a huge frill extending from its head, topped with a series of dangerous-looking spikes. Just for good measure, it also had a 60cm (2ft) spike on top of its snout. No-one would like to be on the receiving end of that.

Ankylosaurus had a very small brain, not much bigger than a lime or lemon. Probably only stegosaurus, the least intelligent of all the dinosaurs, had less grey matter. But, ankylosaurus didn't need a high IQ. All it had to do was munch on plants and squat low and swing its tail if any predator made the mistake of attacking it.

Styracosaurus

ANKYLOSAURUS
Location: North America
Length: 7 metres (23ft)

| Precambrian 4,540-541mya |
| Cambrian 541-485mya |
| Ordovician 485-443 mya |
| Silurian 443-419 mya |
| Devonian 419-359 mya |
| Carboniferous 359-299mya |
| Permian 299-252mya |
| Triassic 252-201mya |
| Jurassic 201-145mya |
| **Cretaceous 145-66mya** |
| Paleogene 66-23mya |
| Neogene 23-2.6mya |
| Quaternary 2.6mya - present |

Did You Know?

Some scientists think styracosaurus would knock down trees with their horns, beak and great weight, then eat the leaves and twigs.

25

KING OF THE DINOSAURS

Check out this battle between two T. rexes. You might have thought they would have picked on smaller animals. But several T. rex bones bear tooth wounds that could only have been made by other T. rexes.

So why did T. rexes fight?

Well, eliminating a rival T. rex would mean you would have an easier time hunting in one area. Or the battle may have been worth fighting over a mate or a scavenged carcass.

Meet the ultimate bone crusher. **Tyrannosaurus rex** was the undisputed king of dinosaurs in the late Cretaceous period. It was up to 6 metres (20ft) tall – about as high as a two-storey house.

Its skull was about 1.5 metres (5ft) long, with the jaws extending to about 1 metre (39in). And those jaws had around 60 teeth, up to 30cm (12in) long. Can you imagine teeth bigger than bananas?

In 2012, scientists tried to work out the force of a T. rex's bite. They found that it was almost 12,800lb, the same as 13 concert grand pianos slamming down on its prey. This makes it the hardest-biting land animal ever known. Megalodon, a giant shark that became extinct about 1.5 million years ago, had the hardest bite at 41,000lb. Deinosuchus, a crocodile that lived in North America at the same time T. rex, also, had a more powerful bite at 23,000lb.

T. rex needed its 30cm (12in) teeth: as scientists estimate that it could bite off 230kg (500lb) of meat. So it's easy to see why it would attack a fellow T. rex – at 7,000kg (7.7 tons), it made for a hearty good meal.

When fighting another T. rex, it would have aimed to clamp down on its opponent's neck or jaws. If it had targeted any other part of the body, it would have been left open to counterattack.

Tyrannosaurus rex

TYRANNOSAURUS REX
Location: North America
Length: About 12.2 metres (40ft)

| Precambrian 4,540-541mya |
| Cambrian 541-485mya |
| Ordovician 485-443 mya |
| Silurian 443-419 mya |
| Devonian 419-359 mya |
| Carboniferous 359-299mya |
| Permian 299-252mya |
| Triassic 252-201mya |
| Jurassic 201-145mya |
| **Cretaceous 145-66mya** |
| Paleogene 66-23mya |
| Neogene 23-2.6mya |
| Quaternary 2.6mya - present |

T. rex wasn't the only cannibal dinosaur. Majungasaurus, which lived in Madagascar 84-70 million years ago, is also known to have eaten its own kind.

Did You Know?

No-one is sure why T. rex's arms were so short. They were probably used for grasping its prey. But they were too short to lift any meat to its mouth – its jaws probably did most of the work!

ASTEROID ATTACK!

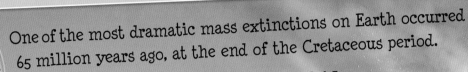

One of the most dramatic mass extinctions on Earth occurred 65 million years ago, at the end of the Cretaceous period.

Over three-quarters of the land animals died out

– as well as all the huge flying reptiles, known as pterosaurs, and all the giant sea reptiles, such as the pliosaurs and mosasaurs. The only dinosaurs to escape the destruction were ones with wings that had evolved into birds.

What's the difference between an asteroid, a meteor and meteorite? An asteroid is a rocky object in space that orbits the sun. Sometimes asteroids enter the Earth's atmosphere and then they are known as meteors. They burn and vaporize, leaving bright streaks in the sky, so meteors are also known as "shooting stars". If a meteor survives the plunge through the atmosphere and lands on the Earth, it's known as a meteorite.

Scientists estimate that the asteroid created an impact about 2 million times greater than the most powerful nuclear bomb ever detonated. It made a crater measuring 150km (93 miles) wide.

Turtles and crocodiles survived the end-Cretaceous extinction, along with smaller animals, such as snails, snakes, amphibians - including salamanders and frogs - and small lizards, inclding iguanas.

Precambrian
4,540-541mya

Cambrian
541-485mya

Ordovician
485-443 mya

Silurian
443-419 mya

Devonian
419-359 mya

Carboniferous
359-299mya

Permian
299-252mya

Triassic
252-201mya

Jurassic
201-145mya

Cretaceous
145-66mya

Paleogene
66-23mya

Neogene
23-2.6mya

Quaternary
2.6mya - present

Dinosaurs had been alive for a staggering 165 million years. So why did they suddenly die out? In 1980, the American scientist Luis Alvarez came up with an answer. He found that rock from the end of the Cretaceous period contained lots of iridium, a metal that is rare on Earth but common in asteroids. This led him to believe that a massive asteroid must have hit the Earth and wiped out the dinosaurs.

The problem? An asteroid would have left a huge crater somewhere. An answer came when, scientists found the Chicxulub (cheek-she-loob) crater on the seabed near Mexico (see above). It had been created by a meteorite 10km (6 miles) wide that threw masses of super-hot dust into the Earth's atmosphere, blocking out the sun.

Without sunlight, many plants died, so the herbivorous dinosaurs had nothing to eat. And without the herbivores, the carnivorous dinosaurs had nothing to eat. The era of the dinosaurs was over.

Did You Know?

The end-Cretaceous extinction was not the only mass extinction in the history of the Earth. There have been five, with the worst at the end of the Permian period, 252 million years ago, when about 95% of all species died out. Scientists think this was caused by huge volcanic eruptions that lasted 600,000 years!

Deinonychus

Pronounced: Day-non-ic-us

Some scientists don't think deinonychus hunted as a team, but that they hunted in a more "selfish" way, like the komodo dragons of Indonesia. These lizards wound their prey with a venomous bite, then let it die. Other komodo dragons are attracted to the smell of the prey and they fight each other when feasting. This could explain how many deinonychus skeletons often appear at the site of a single tenontosaurus. They killed each other to get the best pickings!

Ankylosaurus

Pronounced: Ank-ill-oh-sore-us

By the end of the Cretaceous period, ankylosaurs were among the last dinosaurs standing. Hungry tyrannosaurs couldn't wipe them out, but the huge meteorite that hit the world 65 million years ago did.

Dreadnoughtus

Pronounced: Dread-nort-us

Dreadnoughtus was a type of titanosaur, a group of sauropod vegetarian dinosaurs. Their heads were tiny, even for sauropods, and many, if not all, are believed to have had tough, bony plates covering their bodies. Many were huge like dreadnoughtus itself, and argentinosaurus.

Spinosaurus

Pronounced: Spine-oh-sore-us

In 2014, new fossil finds in Morocco suggested that spinosaurus might have been a good swimmer and hunted sharks. Its nostrils were on top of its crocodile-like skull, so it could breathe when its head was underwater. And it had long feet and large, flat claws, leading experts to deduce it also had webbing between the toes to help with swimming and walking on wet ground.

Quetzalcoatlus

Pronounced: Kwet-zal-co-at-lus

Douglas Lawson, an American geology student, first found the remains of a quetzalcoatlus at Big Bend National Park in Texas in 1971. He named it after the Aztec flying serpent god, Quetzalcoatl.

Oviraptor

Pronounced: Oh-vih-rap-tore

On the second toe of each hind foot, oviraptor had a curved claw, which it used to slash at prey in sudden, surprise attacks. It kept this claw off the ground, and therefore sharp, by walking on its third and fourth toes.

Centrosaurus

Pronounced: Sen-tro-sore-us

The exact diet of the centrosaurus is still unclear. Centrosaurs lived about 77-75 million years ago and grasses only evolved from about 70 million years ago. They probably ate the thick leaves and twigs of cycads and palm trees, and perhaps ferns.

Protoceratops

Pronounced: Pro-toe-ker-ah-tops

Protoceratops is Greek for "first horned face". It was one of the first ceratopsians, a group of beaked herbivorous dinosaurs. Later ceratopsians include such famous dinosaurs as triceratops, centrosaurus and styracosaurus. These dinosaurs were all much bigger than protoceratops.

Tyrannosaurus rex

Pronounced: Ty-ran-o-sore-us rex

Some scientists have claimed that T. rex was only a scavenger, not a hunter - in other words, it did not kill its prey, but fed on carcasses. However, in 2013, American palaeontologist David Burnham found a T. rex tooth in the tail of a vegetarian hadrosaur. The wound had healed and the hadrosaur had survived the attack. This showed that the T. rex had tried to kill a live animal, and therefore was a hunter.

INDEX

THE AUTHOR
Matthew Rake lives in London and has worked in publishing for more than 20 years. He has written on a wide variety of topics, including science, sports and the arts.

THE ARTIST
Peter Minister started out as a special-effects sculptor and had a successful and exciting career producing sculptures and props for museums, theme parks, TV and film. He now works in CGI, which allows him to express himself with a big ball of digital clay in a more creative way than any "real" clay. His CGI dinosaurs and other animals have appeared in numerous books worldwide.